THOUGHTS

FROM

GREAT WOMEN

PATRICIA MARTIN

Glendale Heights, IL 60139

Compiled by Patricia Martin

Cover Design by Design Dynamics
Illustrations by Darrin Thompson
Typeset Design by Bostrom Publishing

Published by Great Quotations, Inc.

Library of Congress Catalog Card Number : 98-075793

ISBN: 1-56245-377-7

Printed in Hong Kong

This book is dedicated to all my friends

who believed in me.

You know who you are.

Anne Frank

1929 - 1945
German/Dutch Diarist

I n spite of everything I still believe that people are really good at heart.

Anne Frank dreamt of being a journalist "and later on a famous writer." Her diary — a present she received on her thirteenth birthday — was a square album bound in red and white checks. In this small book she recorded poetry and stories, along with her hopes, fears, and reflections during the two years she and her family were hiding from Nazi persecution. After her death at the age of 16 in a prison camp, Ms. Frank's memoirs inspired the Pulitzer-prize winning drama, THE DIARY OF ANNE FRANK.

W hoever is happy will make others happy too. He who has courage and faith will never perish in misery!

W e all live with the objective of being happy; our lives are all different and yet the same.

I know I can write, a couple of my stories are good...there's a lot in my diary that speaks, but — whether I have real talent remains to be seen.

I don't think of all the misery but of the beauty that still remains.

I want to go on living even after my death. And therefore I am grateful to God for giving me this gift, this possibility of developing myself and of writing, of expressing all that is in me! I can shake off everything if I write; my sorrows disappear, my courage is reborn!

P arents can only give good advice or put them on the right paths, but the final forming of a person's character lies in their own hands.

Eleanor Roosevelt

1884-1962
American First Lady,
Stateswoman, Humanitarian

History shows that a nation interested primarily in material things invariably is on a downward path.

One of the most inspiring women in American political history, Eleanor Roosevelt lived a life of action and achievement. The niece of Theodore Roosevelt and wife of President Franklin Roosevelt, Mrs. Roosevelt was a political leader in her own right. She served as a delegate to the United Nations general assembly, and helped to draw up the Declaration of Human Rights. A global thinker, she worked ceaselessly on civil rights for U.S. Black-Americans and for human rights worldwide.

The purpose of life, after all, is to live it, to taste experience to the utmost, to reach out eagerly and without fear for newer and richer experience.

I think somehow we learn who we really are, then live with that decision.

A woman is like a tea bag. You never know how strong she is until she gets into hot water.

*Y*ou gain strength, courage, and confidence by every experience in which you really stop to look fear in the face. You are able to say to yourself, "I lived through this horror. I can take the next thing that comes along."...You must do the thing you think you cannot do.

*T*he giving of love is an education in itself.

*L*ife was meant to be lived and curiosity must be kept alive. One must never, for whatever reason, turn his back on life.

Clare Boothe Luce

1903-1987
Diplomat, Politician, Writer

S ince the world began there never was complete equality about anything.

Clare Boothe Luce was a feminist since her school days, and evolved into one of the era's most prominent women. A respected journalist and successful playwright, she travelled to the Far East as Life Magazine's War Correspondent. Later in life, Ms. Boothe Luce served two terms in Congress and was U.S. Ambassador to Italy. Upon her death, TIME magazine hailed her as "the pre-eminent Renaissance woman of the century."

*C*ensorship, like charity, should begin at home; but unlike charity, it should end there.

*T*houghts have no sex.

*T*o be a liberated woman is to renounce the desire of being a sex object or a baby girl. It is to acknowledge that the Cinderella-Prince Charming story is a child's fairy tale.

I may have married for money, but I certainly didn't divorce for it.

We wanted so much of what we had, and we had so much of what we wanted. Why weren't we happy?

A man's home may seem to be his castle on the outside; inside it is more often his nursery.

Until you have heard death scream in a shell or bomb through the insensible air, impersonally seeking you out personally, you never quite believe that you are mortal.

Georgia O'Keefe

1887-1986
Artist

𝒯 he days you work best are the best days.

As an artist, Georgia O'Keefe came of age with American modernism, and proceeded to establish her own unique vision. Best known for her large, semi-abstract studies of flowers and sun-dried animal bones, she divided her time between New York City, upstate New York, and New Mexico. Having experienced the early suffrage movement before World War I, Ms. O'Keefe was profoundly influenced by feminist thought. She was married to the renowned photographer Alfred Stieglitz, and was one of his favorite photographic subjects.

I want real things — music that makes holes in the sky.

I feel there is something unexplored about women that only a woman can explore...

I believe that to create one's own world in any of the arts takes courage.

Where I was born and where and how I have lived is unimportant. It is what I have done with where I have been that should be of interest.

Nobody sees a flower — really — it is so small — we haven't the time — and to see takes time like to have a friend takes time.

The first feeling was hunger for reality and sincerity, a desire for simplicity.

Harriet Beecher Stowe

1811-1896
Writer, Suffragist, Abolitionist

𝒫eople who hate trouble generally get a good deal of it.

Harriet Beecher Stowe was an early feminist and humanitarian who championed for women's rights and the abolishment of slavery. The inspiration for her novel, UNCLE TOM'S CABIN, came to her in a vision in 1848. It was first published as a series in 1851 - 1852, and was immediately successful. Ms. Beecher Stowe's other published works include the New England novels THE MINISTER'S WOOING and OLD-TOWN FOLKS, as well as numerous essays and religious poems.

Women are the architects of society.

Most mothers are instinctive philosophers.

I would not attack the faith of a heathen without being sure I had a better one to put in its place.

When you get into a tight place and everything goes against you, till it seems as though you could not hang on a minute longer, never give up then, for that is just the place and time that the tide will turn.

So much has been said and sung of beautiful young girls, why don't somebody wake up to the beauty of old women?

My soul ain't yours, mas'r! You haven't bought it — ye can't buy it! It's been bought and paid for, by one that is able to keep it.

Pearl S. Buck

1892-1973
Writer, Humanitarian

*L ove cannot be forced...Love
cannot be coaxed and teased.
It comes out of Heaven unmasked
and unsought.*

Both of Pearl Sydenstricker Buck's
parents were missionaries in China,
and she spent her youth — as well as
most of her life — in the East.
Through her novels, which centered
around Chinese life, she hoped to
make the East, its ways, and its
people more understandable to
Westerners. In 1932, Ms. Buck
received a Pulitzer prize for
The Good Earth, and was awarded a
Nobel Prize for Literature in 1938.

All things are possible until they are proved impossible — and even the impossible may only be so as of now.

The secret joy in work is contained in one word — excellence. To know how to do something well is to enjoy it.

I don't wait for moods. You accomplish nothing if you do that. Your mind must know it has got to get down to earth.

I nside myself is a place where I live all alone, and that's where you renew your springs that never dry up.

I have enough for this life. If there is no other life, than this one has been enough to make it worth being born, myself a human being.

Helen Keller

1880-1968
Writer

L ife is either a daring adventure or nothing.

For the first 19 months of her life, Helen Keller was a happy, active, normal child...Then a high fever robbed her of her sight and hearing. The world turned dark and silent until her teacher and friend, Anne Sullivan, helped her learn to read, write, and speak. Ms. Keller graduated with honors from Radcliffe College in Massachusetts, and spent her adult life bettering the conditions of hearing-impaired and vision-impaired people. Her biography, <u>The Story Of My Life</u>, has inspired generations of readers.

No pessimist ever discovered the secrets of the stars, or sailed to an uncharted land, or opened a new heaven to the human spirit.

Avoiding danger is no safer in the long run than outright exposure. The fearful are caught as often as the bold.

I long to accomplish a great and noble task, but it is my chief duty to accomplish small tasks as if they were great and noble.

To keep our faces toward change and behave like free spirits in the presence of fate is strength undefeatable.

When indeed shall we learn that we are all related one to the other, that we are all members of one body? Until the spirit of love for our fellowmen, regardless of race, color, or creed, shall fill the world, making real in our lives and our deeds the actuality of human brotherhood — until the great mass of the people shall be filled with the sense of responsibility for each other's welfare, social justice can never be attained.

Maya Angelou

Born 1928
Author, Poet, Playwright, Actress

If one is lucky, a solitary fantasy can totally transform one million realities.

Born Marguerite Johnson, Maya Angelou is a prolific novelist, poet, playwright, short story author, and performer. Her series of moving autobiographical works describe the struggle of a southern Black woman seeking physical and spiritual liberation. Ms. Angelou has numerous stage and screen writing credits, including original screenplay and musical score for the film GEORGIA, GEORGIA. She is presently Reynolds Professor at Wake Forest University, Winston-Salem, North Carolina.

S elf-pity in its early stages is as snug as a feather mattress. Only when it hardens does it become uncomfortable.

A cynical young person is almost the saddest sight to see, because it means that he or she has gone from knowing nothing to believing nothing.

T he loss of young first love is so painful that it borders on the ludicrous.

Few, if any, survive their teens.
Most surrender to the vague
but murderous pressure of
adult conformity.

Even minimal people can't
survive on minimal wage.

I note the obvious differences
between each sort and type,
but we are more alike, my friends,
than we are unalike.

Gloria Steinem

Born 1934
Journalist, Writer, Feminist

S elf-esteem isn't everything; it's just that there's nothing without it.

Intelligent, witty, and charismatic, Gloria Steinem was a leading personality of the women's movment during the volatile 1960's. A highly visible journalist, feminist, and humanitarian, she was actively involved in protest campaigns against racism and the Vietnam War. In addition, Ms. Steinem co-founded the Women's Action Alliance and Ms. Magazine — a ground-breaking publication described as a "how-to magazine for the liberated female human being — not how to make jelly but how to seize control of your life."

he moment we find the reason behind an emotion...the wall we have built is breached, and the positive memories it has kept from us return, too. That is why it pays to ask those painful questions. The answers can set you free.

ny woman who chooses to behave like a full human being should be warned that armies of the status quo will treat her as something of a dirty joke; that's their natural and first weapon.

The Golden Rule works for men as written, but for women it should go the other way around. We need to do unto ourselves as we do unto others.

I can sometimes deal with men as equals and therefore can afford to like them.

Hope is a very unruly emotion.

But for me, security is not knowing what's going to happen. Because if I don't know, it could be terrific.

Virginia Woolf

1882-1941
English Writer, Critic

It is far harder to kill a phantom than a reality.

The NEW YORK TIMES has called Virginia Woolf "one of the most subtle, original and modern of moderns, herself a born writer." A master of the novel and essay, Ms. Woolf was considered one of the best literary critics of her time. In her novels, essays, and speeches, she explored such issues as economic independence for women and the tensions of wanting both marriage and a career. She is distinguished by her perceptive *stream of consciousness* literary voice.

For most of history, anonymous was a woman.

Women have served all these centuries as looking glasses possessing the magic and delicious power of reflecting the figure of man at twice its natural size.

Anything may happen when womanhood has ceased to be a protected occupation.

I ncessant company is as bad as
solitary confinement.

T hose comfortably padded
lunatic asylums which are known,
euphemistically, as the stately
homes of England.

B e truthful, one would say, and
the result is bound to be amazingly
interesting. Comedy is bound to be
enriched. New facts are bound to
be discovered.

Oprah Winfrey

Born 1954
Talk Show Host, Actress

When I look into the future, it's so bright it burns my eyes.

NEWSDAY columnist Marvin Kitman has called Oprah "a real person in the fake world of TV." In 1987, THE OPRAH WINFREY SHOW was awarded the Emmy as television's best talk show, and Ms. Winfrey herself received an Emmy for best talk show host. In addition, she has been honored with nominations for both Academy and Golden Globe awards for her portrayal of the character *Sofia* in THE COLOR PURPLE. Fearless, spontaneous, warm, and witty, Ms. Winfrey is an inspiration to millions of women around the country.

*D*oing the best at this moment puts you in the best place for the next moment.

*L*uck is a matter of preparation meeting opportunity.

*I*t isn't until you come to a spiritual understanding of who you are — not necessarily a religious feeling, but deep down, the spirit within — that you can begin to take control.

*U*nless you choose to do great things with it, it makes no difference how much you are rewarded, or how much power you have.

I have a lot of things to prove
to myself. One is that I can live my
life fearlessly.

D ishing the dirt and meddling
in other folks's business is what
I do best.

S ure I was a token. But honey,
I was one happy token.

W e go to the heart of the matter.
We go for the absolute gut.

Anaïs Nin

1903-1977
American/French Writer

𝓛 iving never wore one out so much as the effort not to live.

Anais Nin was born in Paris in 1903, and travelled to New York when she was nine-years-old. Her famous DIARY — which consists of more than 150 volumes — began as a letter she wrote to her father on her voyage to America. Her first book, D.H. LAWRENCE: AN UNPROFESSIONAL STUDY, was the first critique of the author by a woman. Later, Ms. Nin wrote erotica — at a dollar a page — for a *book collector* who had initially approached her friend Henry Miller. As a woman ahead of her time, Anais Nin created the feminine voice of sensuality.

There are very few human beings who receive the truth, complete and staggering, by instant illumination. Most of us acquire it fragment by fragment, on a small scale, by successive developments, cellularly, like a laborious mosaic.

The artist is not there to be at one with the world, he is there to transform it.

We don't see things as they are, we see things as we are.

The dream was always running ahead of one. To catch up, to live for a moment in unison with it, that was the miracle.

I will not be just a tourist in the world of images, just watching images passing by which I cannot live in, make love to, possess as permanent sources of joy and ecstasy.

Anne Morrow Lindbergh

Born 1906
Writer

$\mathcal{O}$ ne should lie empty, open, choiceless as a beach — waiting for a gift from the sea.

Anne Morrow Lindbergh's life has been a unique blend of high adventure, sudden change, and domesticity. The wife of aviator Charles Lindbergh, she accompanied her husband on numerous flights as copilot, navigator, radio operator, photographer, and log keeper. The tragic kidnapping and murder of their first son in 1932 led to passing of "The Lindbergh Act." In the following years, Ms. Lindbergh raised five children and continued to write her inspiring books.

W hat a comment on civilization, when being alone is considered suspect; when one has to apologize for it, make excuses, hide the fact that one practices it — like a secret vice.

I t is terribly amusing how many climates of feelings one can go through in one day.

S ecurity in a relationship lies neither in looking back to what was in nostalgia, nor forward to what it might be in dread or anticipation, but living in the present relationship and accepting it as it is now.

I ...understand why the saints were rarely married woman. I am convinced it has nothing to do, as I once supposed, with chastity or children. It has to do primarily with distractions. Women's normal occupations in general run counter to the creative life, or contemplative life, or saintly life.

*E*ven those whose lives had appeared to be ticking impeturbably under their smiling clock-faces were often trying, like me, to evolve another rhythm with more creative pauses in it, more adjustment to their individual needs and new and more alive relationships to themselves as well as others.

Mother Teresa

Born 1910-1996
Roman Catholic Missionary

*We can do no great things —
only small things with great love.*

Born Agnes Bojaxhiu in the Albanian town of Skopje, she was known worldwide as *Mother Teresa* — a seeming angel on earth who cared for the sick, poor, and hungry of Calcutta. She entered the convent at age 18, and became an Indian citizen in 1948. Founder of the Missionaries of Charity, Mother Teresa received the Nobel Peace Prize in 1979. She said "God has called me not to be successful, he has called me to be faithful." Her selfless giving touched the lives of many people as she served as an inspiring example of the power of faith.

Joy is a net of love by which you can catch souls.

Kind words can be short and easy to speak, but their echoes are truly endless.

Loneliness and the feeling of being unwanted is the most terrible poverty.

Holiness consists of doing the will of God with a smile.

I have found the paradox that if
I love until it hurts, then there is no
hurt, but only more love.

A beautiful death is for people
who have lived like animals to die
like angels.

T o keep a lamp burning we have
to keep putting oil in it.

G od is the friend of silence.
Trees, flowers, grass grow in silence.
See the stars, moon, and sun,
how they move in silence.

Golda Meir

1898-1978
Russian-American Israeli Politician

$\mathcal{D}$on't be humble; you're not that great.

Golda Meir was born in Russia, and emigrated to American shores in 1906, at the age of eight. She went to Palestine in 1921, and is a founder of the republic of Israel. Politically active and outspoken, Ms. Meir served as foreign minister from 1956 to 1966, and became Israel's fourth prime minister in 1969. Upset over the 1973 Arab-Israeli War led to election loses for Labor and, unable to form a government, Ms. Meir resigned in 1974.

We only want that which is given
naturally to all peoples of the world,
to be masters of our own fate, only
of our own fate, not of others, and
in cooperation and friendship
with others.

I must govern the clock, not be
governed by it.

At work, you think of the
children you have left at home. At
home, you think of the work you've
left unfinished. Such a struggle is
unleashed within yourself.
Your heart is rent.

*T*hose who do not know how to weep with their whole heart don't know how to laugh either.

*T*o be successful, a woman has to be better at her job than a man.

*I*f you knew how often I say to myself: to hell with everything, to hell with everybody, I've done my share, let the others do theirs now, enough, enough, enough.

*O*ld age is like a plane flying through a storm. Once you're aboard, there's nothing you can do.

N o woman should be shamefaced in attempting, through her work, to give back to the world a portion of its lost heart.

Louise Bogan

" *Y* es," I answered you last night;
"No," this morning, sir, I say:
Colors seen by candlelight
Will not look the same by day.

Elizabeth Barrett Browning

I t's not love's going that hurts my days — but that it went in little ways.

Edna St. Vincent Millay

S ince when was genius found respectable?

Elizabeth Barrett Browning

It's never to late too be what you might have been.

George Eliot

It had long since come to my attention that people of accomplishment rarely sat back and let things happen to them. They went out and happened to things.

Elinor Smith

Genius, whether locked up in a cell or roaming at large, is always solitary...

George Sand

She would not exchange her solitude for anything. Never again to be forced to move to the rhythms of others.

Tillie Olsen

Dreams have only one owner at a time. That's why dreamers are lonely.

Erma Bombeck

Don't be afraid your life will end; be afraid that it will never begin.

Grace Hansen

How many cares one loses when one decides not to be something, but to be someone.

Coco (Gabrielle) Chanel

There are two ways of spreading light: to be the candle or the mirror that reflects it.

Edith Wharton

Creative minds have always been known to survive any kind of bad training.

Anna Freud

You were once wild here. Don't let them tame you!

Isadora Duncan

No one worth possessing can be quite possessed.

Sara Teasdale

Living is a form of not being sure,
not knowing what is next or how.
The moment you know, you begin to
die a little. The artist never entirely
knows. We guess. We may be
wrong, but we take leap after leap
in the dark.

Agnes De Mille

My candle burns at both ends;
It will not last the night;
But, ah, my foes, and oh, my friends
— It gives a lovely light.

Edna St. Vincent Millay

Exhaust the little moment.
Soon it dies. And be it gash or gold,
it will not come again in this
identical disguise.

Gwendolyn Brooks

I t seems to me we can never give up longing and wishing while we are alive. There are certain things we feel to be beautiful and good, and we must hunger for them.

George Eliot

N ature has created us with the capacity to know God, to experience God.

Alice Walker

W hen will women begin to have the first glimmer that above all other loyalties is the loyalty to truth, i.e., to yourself, that husband, children, friends, and country are as nothing to that?

Alice James

Think wrongly, if you please, but in all cases think for yourself.

Doris Lessing

There are many realities. We should remember this when we get too caught in being concerned about the way the rest of the world lives or how we think they live.

Natalie Goldberg

I'll walk where my own nature would be leading; it vexes me to choose another guide.

Emily Bronte

I've done more harm by the falseness of trying to please than by the honesty of trying to hurt.

Jessamyn West

*T*rue feeling justifies whatever it may cost.

May Sarton

*W*hat's terrible is to pretend that the second-rate is first-rate.
To pretend that you don't need love when you do; or that you like your work when you know quite well that you're capable of better.

Doris Lessing

*A*nd the trouble is, if you don't risk anything, you risk even more.

Erica Jong

*L*ife's under no obligation to give us what we expect.

Margaret Mitchell

Y ou live. No use asking whether life will bring you pleasure or unhappiness, whether it will prove a blessing or a curse. Who could answer these questions? You live, you breathe.

George Sand

F ate keeps on happening.

Anita Loos

S he wants to live for once. But doesn't know quite what that means. Wonders if she has ever done it. If she ever will.

Alice Walker

C reativity can be described as letting go of certainties.

Gail Sheehy

Invention, it must be humbly admitted, does not consist of creating out of void, but out of chaos.

Mary Sheeley

For years I have endeavored to calm an impetuous tide — laboring to make my feelings take an orderly course — it was striving against the stream.

Mary Wollstonecraft

It's better to die on your feet than to live on your knees.

Dolores Ibarruri

I think that wherever your journey takes you, there are new gods waiting there, with divine patience — and laughter.

Susan M. Watkins

T he woman who has sprung free has emotional mobility. She is able to move toward the things that are satisfying to her and away from those that are not. She is free, also, to succeed.

Colette Dowling

I 'll not listen to reason ... Reason always means what someone else has got to say.

Elizabeth Cleghorn Gaskell

There are no more thorough prudes than those women who have some little secret to hide.

George Sand

Conventionality is not morality. Self-righteousness is not religion.

Charlotte Bronte

Prejudices...are most difficult to eradicate from the heart whose soil has never been loosened or fertilized by education: they grow there, firm as weeds among stones.

Charlotte Bronte

A patronizing disposition always has its meaner side.

George Eliot

Honeyed words like bees, gilded and sticky, with a little sting.

Elinor Hoyt Wylie

The only sin passion can commit is to be joyless.

Dorothy Sayers

You will do foolish things, but do them with enthusiasm.

Colette

Anger as soon fed is dead
'Tis starving makes it fat.

Emily Dickinson

The main dangers in this life are the people who want to change everything...or nothing.

Lady Astor

One can remain alive long past the usual date of disintegration if one is unafraid of change, insatiable in intellectual curiosity, interested in big things, and happy in small ways.

Edith Wharton

I have accepted fear as a part of life — specifically the fear of change ... I have gone ahead despite the pounding in the heart that says: turn back.

Erica Jong

No idea is so antiquated that it was not once modern. No idea is so modern that it will not someday be antiquated.

Ellen Glasgow

The story of a love is not important — what is important is that one is capable of love. It is perhaps the only glimpse we are permitted of eternity.

Helen Hayes

Nobody has ever measured, not even poets, how much the heart can hold.

Zelda Fitzgerald

Chains do not hold a marriage together. It is threads, hundreds of tiny threads, which sew people together through the years.

Simone Signoret

What is most beautiful in virile men is something feminine; what is most beautiful in feminine women is something masculine.

Susan Sontag

Manners are a sensitive awareness of the feelings of others. If you have that awareness, you have good manners, no matter what fork you use.

Emily Post

There are people who have money and people who are rich.

Coco (Gabrielle) Chanel

Tact is after all a kind of mind-reading.

Sarah Orne Jewette

O ur "pathway" is straight to the ballot box, with no variableness nor shadow of turning...

Elizabeth Cady Stanton

W oman stock is rising in the market. I shall not live to see women vote, but I'll come and rap at the ballot box.

Lydia Marie Child

T he single most impressive fact about the attempt by American women to obtain the right to vote is how long it took.

Alice Schaerr Rossi

G reat men can't be ruled.

Ayn Rand

Other Titles by Great Quotations, Inc.

Hard Covers

Ancient Echoes
Behold the Golfer
Commanders in Chief
The Essence of Music
First Ladies
Good Lies for Ladies
Great Quotes From Great Teachers
Great Women
Thought of You Today
Journey to Success
Just Between Friends
Lasting Impressions
My Husband My Love
Never Ever Give Up
The Passion of Chocolate
Peace Be With You
The Perfect Brew
The Power of Inspiration
Sharing the Season
Teddy Bears
There's No Place Like Home

Paperbacks

301 Ways to Stay Young
ABC's of Parenting
Angel-grams
African American Wisdom
Astrology for Cats
Astrology for Dogs
The Be-Attitudes
Birthday Astrologer
Can We Talk
Chocoholic Reasonettes
Cornerstones of Success
Daddy & Me
Erasing My Sanity
Graduation is Just the Beginning
Grandma I Love You
Happiness is Found Along the Way
Hooked on Golf
Ignorance is Bliss
In Celebration of Women
Inspirations
Interior Design for Idiots

Great Quotations, Inc.
1967 Quincy Court
Glendale Heights,IL 60139 USA
Phone: 630-582-2800   Fax: 630-582-2813
http://www.greatquotations.com

Other Titles by Great Quotations, Inc.

Paperbacks

I'm Not Over the Hill
Life's Lessons
Looking for Mr. Right
Midwest Wisdom
Mommy & Me
Mother, I Love You
The Mother Load
Motivating Quotes
Mrs.Murphy's Laws
Mrs. Webster's Dictionary
Only A Sister
The Other Species
Parenting 101
Pink Power
Romantic Rhapsody
The Secret Langauge of Men
The Secret Langauge of Women
The Secrets in Your Name
A Servant's Heart
Social Disgraces
Stress or Sanity
A Teacher is Better Than
Teenage of Insanity
Touch of Friendship
Wedding Wonders
Words From the Coach

Perpetual Calendars

365 Reasons to Eat Chocolate
Always Remember Who Loves Yo
Best Friends
Coffee Breaks
The Dog Ate My Car Keys
Extraordinary Women
Foundations of Leadership
Generations
The Heart That Loves
The Honey Jar
I Think My Teacher Sleeps at Scho
I'm a Little Stressed
Keys to Success
Kid Stuff
Never Never Give Up
Older Than Dirt
Secrets of a Successful Mom
Shopoholic
Sweet Dreams
Teacher Zone
Tee Times
A Touch of Kindness
Apple a Day
Golf Forever
Quotes From Great Women
Teacher Are First Class